# HOW TO
# HEAR
# THE VOICE

# GOD

## AND
## UNDERSTAND
## IT

# ALSO BY ADAM HOUGE

*The 7 Most Powerful Prayers That
Will Change Your Life Forever*

*How To Hear The Voice Of God And Understand It*

*How To Memorize The Bible Quick
And Easy In 5 Simple Steps*

*How To Memorize The Entire Bible In No Time Flat*

*Choosing Words That Heal*

*The Power and The Passion*

*I Know That God Is Good
But Why Am I hurting So Much*

*Increasing Your Faith Beyond Mustard Seed*

ADAM HOUGE

# HOW TO HEAR THE VOICE *of* GOD AND UNDERSTAND IT

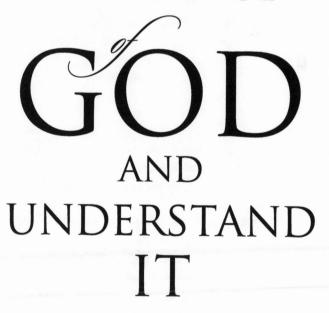

# CONTENTS

Introduction............................... 7

*Understanding His Voice Through Conviction* .. 9

*Conforming Our Hearts to His* ..............15

*Tugging at Our Hearts* .....................33

*The Unrealized Influence of God* .............41

*Having Passion for Christ*...................53

# INTRODUCTION

G OD SPEAKS TO us in many ways: through the circumstances of life, through the issues of the heart,
through His Holy Spirit, and in His word. When we
understand how the inward voice of God works, it is
easier to understand His will and His outward voice. The
outward voice of God is a leading of the Lord through
open and closed doors, circumstances, and various fruits
of life. It can be difficult to discern His leading and His
will for us if we don't know how to discern the inward
speech of the Holy Spirit.

# UNDERSTANDING HIS VOICE THROUGH CONVICTION

WE ARE CREATURES of the flesh. Weak, we came from a background of sin and struggle with temptation. God gave us His Holy Spirit to establish us in the foundation of Jesus Christ that through Christ, we may no longer know sin but walk in righteousness. Due to our sinful nature, conviction is the most widely known voice of the Holy Spirit.

Every Christian has conviction, but not every Christian always obeys conviction. If we always obeyed conviction, we would never have sin. Sometimes the issue of sin can be in regard to recognizing conviction when we're caught up in the heat of the tempting moment. The desire of the flesh plagues us like an evil thing. It tears at us with a gnawing fury. But the Holy Spirit was sent to us to deliver us from the slavery of sin through the saving grace of Jesus Christ.

If we do not listen to the Holy Spirit but walk in a pattern of sin, we will continue to be slaves to sin. But if we obey the conviction of the Spirit, His conviction will become easier to understand and clearer to hear. His voice will be easier to obey because He strengthens us to overcome temptation. When He sees our heart, after having tested us, He strengthens us through His power to overcome. If we allow our bodies to rule over us and do not overcome them, we will be trapped by sin and left with a broken relationship between us and the Lord.

If we do not obey conviction, then it becomes more difficult to hear the Spirit. This happens because we allow our flesh to have the louder voice. But if we silence our flesh through meditating on the presence of the Spirit, the voice of God becomes louder and easier to obey. Conviction comes as a still small voice. Rather than being heavy, many times a light conviction is given for the sake of testing.

If we were always heavily convicted, we would not obey sin. But through light conviction, it gives opportunity for free will. God is a God of free will. He's given us the ability to make our own decisions in life and has given us the freedom to think. But if we misuse this freedom, it leads to death. If we put freedom to the test, we will be made slaves to sin. But if we submit to freedom by obedience to the Holy Spirit, freedom will be stronger and will lead to life.

In Christ, we have two natures. We have the nature of the flesh, which is the old creation, and the nature of the Spirit, which is a new creation. In Christ Jesus, we are a new creation, yet we have the old man to deal with in regard to desire, sin, and temptation. Consider these two creations like two separate creatures. One is a harmless child, and the other is a ruthless beast. If we do not tame the beast of the flesh, it will tear apart the young child of Christ in us. If we do not bring our own bodies under subjection, we will not find the freedom being a child of God brings.

Whichever nature you feed the most will become the strongest. If you had the choice between feeding a ruthless beast or your child, which one would you feed? Your own child no doubt. That way your child may grow strong while the beast withers so that it won't harm your child. But if you feed the beast, it will grow strong, and in between feedings, its appetite will grow larger.

If you feed the flesh, the flesh will become a terrifying beast that will overtake you. But if you feed the new creation of Christ in you, it will grow strong while the flesh will grow weak. This is why some struggle with bondage, while others walk in freedom. It's not that some men are stronger in Christ than others, but rather, they know and confess their weaknesses while seeking God for strength. They feed their inner spiritual creation rather than the flesh and thus become more spiritual.

The more you feed the flesh with its desires and act in the flesh to sin, the more its appetite will grow between feedings. Its appetite is temptation, and the more you feed it, the bigger its "stomach" becomes. As a result, the appetite of temptation will grow stronger, and conviction will grow weaker.

If you want more conviction in life, then sit in the presence of the Spirit more, and do not obey the flesh. When you're faithful to listen to Him, you will feel His conviction more frequently and stronger. Why would this be? Because God speaks more frequently to those who listen and obey.

Think about it: who would you rather talk to—someone who doesn't listen to you or care about what you're saying or someone who is all ears, a person who always wants to listen to everything you say and is absorbed in your every word? You'd rather speak to someone who cares about you no doubt! Likewise, God speaks more frequently to those who listen and less to those who turn a deaf ear to Him.

God commands us to listen to and obey His voice. Faith comes by hearing the word of God, and salvation comes through faith. We are saved by His word, and hence we read that we find His mercy when we incline our ears. As it is written,

> "Incline your ear, and come to Me. Hear, and your soul shall live; And I will make an everlasting covenant with you— The sure mercies of David."
>
> Isaiah 55:3

But that we are commanded to obey His voice is evident. For it is written,

> "You shall walk after the LORD your God and fear Him, and keep His commandments and obey His voice; you shall serve Him and hold fast to Him."

DEUTERONOMY 13:4

We must obey the inward voice of the Holy Spirit. We must obey His convictions if we love the Lord. Love fulfills the law. It's not that we need to practice the law, but by walking in love, we will automatically fulfill the law. If you love someone, you will listen to them and care about their words. If you love the Lord, you will listen to Him and care about His words. Knowing that He is your master, you will be careful to apply His words.

Walk in conviction, and the more you listen to it, the more you'll have it. When conviction is stronger, it is easier to overcome sin and bondage. Sometimes it can be difficult to recognize conviction, especially in the heat of a tempting moment. Most of the time, it's because we are closing our ears to God rather than opening them.

Learn to tune your ears inwardly and listen intently for the words of the Spirit. When we intently listen inwardly for His words, we are caring about what He has to say. When we care about what He has to say, we will hear more loudly, more powerfully, and more frequently. In this, conviction will be very strong, by which we will walk in love, faith, and purity.

# CONFORMING
# OUR HEARTS
# TO HIS

GOD CALLS US to be conformed to His image. It is how we were originally created and what we must do. But in order to be His eternal image, first we must conform to His internal image. That is to say, we must conform to the image of the Father conveyed to us through the Holy Spirit, who abides in the inward person.

There are two different types of desires: evil desires and good desires. Evil desires are of the flesh, whereas good desire is of the Spirit. Temptation is born when desire has been conceived. Just as it is written,

> "But each one is tempted when he is drawn away by his own desires and enticed.
> Then, when desire has conceived, it gives birth to sin; and sin, when it is full-grown, brings forth death."
>
> JAMES 1:14–15

Therefore we must be careful what we desire and choose not to follow our own hearts. In following our hearts, we are following a pattern of sin. But in following the heart of Christ, we are following a pattern of righteousness. Not all desire leads to temptation, but all desire can be used for temptation. Even desire for godliness can be used for temptation. For example, if you desire to be a pastor, you desire good work. But if you haven't been called by God to become a pastor yet step out to do so, your desire is not good. Why? Because your desire is of your own heart and not that of the Holy Spirit. You desire a godly thing yet haven't been called to that work.

The work you desire is good, but the desire is not good. You're desiring godliness, but because you are not called by God, and it is not your spiritual gift, your work is not godly. You shouldn't become a pastor without being led, seeing that it is a gift of the Holy Spirit. As it is written,

> "And He Himself gave some to be apostles, some prophets, some evangelists, and some pastors and teachers, for the equipping of the saints for the work of ministry, for the edifying of the body of Christ."
>
> EPHESIANS 4:11–12

Let God give it to you, and do not try to take from the hand of God. Remember that "He Himself gives." This goes the same for many circumstances in life. We must be led by the Lord in all things, following the tugs of the Holy Spirit on our heart.

But if we allow God to change our desires and conform them to His, we will continually work out godliness. Why? Because everything we will desire will be godly. When God leads us, He conforms our heart to His, our will to His, and hence His desires will become our desires.

The closer we are to Him in a relationship, the closer our hearts will be to Him. But seeking Him is more than reading His word and growing in it. It is practicing His word, meditating on it, and memorizing it while also meditating on the leading and presence of the Spirit.

When we grow in understanding, the word we will be closer to Him. Yet when we practice His word, we become like Him. Therefore it is important not only to know the word and the exact meaning of Christ's doctrine but also how to appropriately apply it.

The only way to appropriately apply the doctrine of Christ is through the operation of the Holy Spirit. As the Spirit operates in us and works through us, we work out the gospel by faith. God is always working, and He cannot sin nor does He contradict Himself. Therefore if we let God work through us, we shall not contradict Him nor shall we sin.

Now the question remains, "How can we have Him work through us more?" Simple. By seeking the Spirit and sitting in His presence, we are able to hear Him more clearly. When we hear Him more clearly, we will have opportunity for working out faith, and hence He will work through us.

But when we hear His voice, we need to be diligent to obey immediately. When He pulls at our hearts, we must always obey every time. When we give earnest heed to obeying Him, He will conform our desires to His and our hearts to His. Then with our desire being like His, He can lead us through the desires of His heart.

For example, if you see someone in the church who is poor and struggling, there are two kinds of responses one may have. The first response is "I care about this person, but if I help them, either my family or I will suffer. I need to take care of my family too." Then the second response is "I don't know how, but I need to do something for this person."

Whether you can afford it or not is irrelevant. If you seek something hard enough, you'll find it. Doesn't Jesus exhort us to ask, seek, and knock? How much more will He answer you if you are seeking to provide for someone else? What will God give to you if you ask Him for the help you need to help someone else? If someone needs a home and you don't have a way to provide it, what will God do for you if you ask Him to help you help them? Will He abandon your request? Or will He see your heart and be pleased to work through you?

Don't you believe that He will use you as a tool to deliver someone from their suffering without denting you? But even if you are dented to help another, won't

God help you? If God is calling you to sacrifice, He will provide. Even as we read,

> "And Abraham called the name of the place, The-LORD-Will-Provide; as it is said to this day, 'In the Mount of the LORD it shall be provided.'"
>
> GENESIS 22:14

The original Hebrew name for "The-LORD-Will-Provide" is "Jehovah Jireh." He was called this by Abraham because He provided a sacrifice to spare the life of Isaac. Similarly, God will spare you and your family if He has called you to sacrifice to save your brethren. He is only asking you to sacrifice that He may test your faith. Then when you have been faithful, He will deliver you also. If we step out without being called directly by God to do so, He may not provide. But if the Lord has spoken, He will make good on promises.

If He is not providing you directly with what you need, then perhaps He's calling you to use a different means to save this person. Perhaps He wants you to search the church directory of phone numbers and bring together the hands that can restore this person.

For those of you who are parents, imagine two of your children when they were younger. Consider now from the parent's perspective: if one child was sad and crying and the other one wanted to have compassion on them and came to you and told you they wanted to comfort them, then if they explained that they didn't have what they needed to do so and they asked you for something to bless their brokenhearted sibling, what would you do? Would you tell them no, or would you encourage the bond of kinship between the two of them by providing what they needed to love one another perfectly?

Even so, God will provide when we ask Him for providence. But we should also pray that He would provide for others, not only through our hands but His as well. We should pray that He will provide for our churches, for ministries, for others' families, for brothers and sisters in Christ, and for ourselves. God will give us what we need to give to others, and He gives us what we need to be taken care of ourselves.

Therefore we should always walk by faith. One desire is the desire of the flesh: "I should help but don't have the resources, so I won't." And the other desire is of the Spirit: "I should help, and I know that God has the resources. I will seek the Lord for providence, and I will give to them from God, to God."

We receive from the Lord to sacrifice to the Lord even as Abraham did. He provides for everything we have, and all that we have is His. Therefore have the heart that from God it came and to God it shall return.

In this, the Lord is glorified. Be sensitive to these desires that He lays in your heart and be obedient to them. The desires He lays in your heart require an act of faith. Be ready to step out in faith, but never step out in haste. Pray before anything, and give God an opportunity to confirm His will to you. Not every desire we have is from God, even when it seems good. But as it is written,

> "Be anxious for nothing, but in everything by prayer and supplication, with thanksgiving, let your requests be made known to God."
>
> PHILIPPIANS 4:6

Pray first, and when God confirms His will to you, step out in faith. Step outside of your comfort zone into the place that doesn't make sense and into the place of the difficult seas. If Jesus has called you into the seas, then you will walk on the water. If Jesus has not called you into the seas, you will not walk on water. Remember that before Peter walked on water, first God commanded him to come out on the waves.

Therefore it is good to discern between the Lord's heart and our own desire. God will always tell you what you should do, yet sometimes He doesn't tell you until you ask Him first. Sometimes a needy person is laid at your feet and you hear nothing from God. But this situation is fruit from God for you to work, then after you have prayed, He reveals not only His will to you but the most effective way to help this person.

When we know His will, we ought to be obedient to it. When we obey the Lord, He conforms our heart to His that His desires will become our desires and thus we become more like God. Then in certain circumstances of life, He will lead us by the desires *He* lays in our heart through the Holy Spirit. Yet all things should be confirmed through prayer. Even if you think the desire is laid on your heart from God, you must never be hasty but pray first. If God has laid something in your heart, after you inquire of the Lord, He will show you exactly what He wants you to do and how to do it. But if it doesn't come to fruition, then God never laid it on your heart.

The Holy Spirit will also tug at your heart to lead you, and sometimes He lays a desire on your heart. For example, He presses the desire in your heart to grow in the word. He also presses the desire in your heart to become more involved in church or in fellowship. These are similar to the tugs He gives us on our heart, and they go hand in hand. But it is good to note there are two types of tugs: one that represents the compelling speech of the Spirit and one that is His desire laid on our hearts. The former can always be followed without prayer, but the latter requires prayer first. Why doesn't the speech of the Spirit need prayer? Because He has already spoken, and faith comes by His word. Why do desires require prayer? Because desire is not the word of God, and faith comes by hearing the word of God.

Therefore, beloved, be diligent to lay all things before the Lord in regard to desire. Yet God does press His desire in our hearts to augment His active leading that we should be more willing to obey.

An example of my own life would be in regard to my marriage. When I was younger in the Lord, I considered being single for the Lord. As time went on, He began to press the desire in my heart for a companion. When the desire was first pressed in my heart, it wasn't specific about marriage. It was only a desire for a companion, which could have meant anything. So because I didn't understand, I often prayed for a brother or a friend who would never leave but would always be a part of my life.

Ultimately, that's what he laid in my heart: to have a friend who never left my side. The reality of life is that friends move away or move on with life. Eventually we move away or are called to a different church or ministry, and thus we continue to be grafted to a new part of the body.

As time went on, God increased this desire for a companion and made it more specific: someone who I could continually share the Lord with, edifying in Christ and being edified by. Then shortly before I met my wife, He pressed it in my heart to have a family and be married. I surrendered to Him at this point: "Lord, if it is your desire for me to be married, I lay it at Your feet. I will not seek it, but I pray that you will lead me to it. Father, if this is what you are telling me that you want me to do, then I pray that you will give me one of your daughters' hands in marriage." A few short months after I prayed that prayer, I met my wife. I never dated, never kissed, never did anything with a woman nor did I intend to for my whole life. I was dedicated to the Lord, but He had different plans for me.

Now, I'm not claiming that my circumstance is how He will lead everyone to their spouse. So for those of you still seeking, I do exhort that you pray, and God will lead you in His own way. Yet the point to this example is to discuss the specific nature of desire laid in our hearts by the Lord. I wasn't led by desire, as I chose not to seek a spouse. Rather, the desire He lays in our hearts augments His leading. He does this to help us make righteous decisions.

For example, if you enjoy and desire sin, how will you be broken by the cross? But God breaks us just before we receive Christ as Savior. Thus when we're broken properly, we find conviction, and through conviction, we hate sin. By the hatred of sin and the desire for a new life, we find repentance and a relationship with Christ.

God leads us through our heart cords. Sometimes He tugs on them as we mentioned earlier, and sometimes He plants the seed of His desire to augment that tug. As we continually sit in the presence of the Spirit and practice His word, He changes our desires to conform them to His.

Now let me make something clear: DO NOT BE LED BY DESIRE! I am not teaching that you should be led by desire but merely explaining how God changes our hearts to communicate His will to us. Anytime a desire enters your heart, bring it to God before you do anything. Lay it at His feet and be anxious for nothing, but wait for His answer.

Be objective to His will. When you lay your desires at His feet, let go of them. If you're desiring the wrong thing, it may be difficult to hear the right thing coming from God's mouth. This can happen when you're led by desire or swallowed up in it. Yet the Lord doesn't call us to be swallowed up with desire but to overcome desire through surrendering to Him. In surrender, He can conform our heart to His then, by desire, He may augment the communication of His will to us.

In this, God leads us through desire. Although desire is the beginning of temptation, there is a difference between holy desire and evil desire. Holy, godly desire is the desire of the Holy Spirit at work in your heart. Evil desire is the desire of the flesh at work in your heart.

By making this distinction and pursuing spiritual desire, we can become more pleasing to the Lord. Desire is a method God uses to augment His leading, but it is not a method we can depend upon to be led by. And why? Because of our own hearts. Our own hearts tend to get in the way, and there are times that it can be difficult to make the distinction between our heart and God's heart. If we follow our own heart, we follow the will of the flesh and work out sin. And as it is written,

> "The heart is deceitful above all things, And desperately wicked; Who can know it?"
>
> JEREMIAH 17:9

Therefore, seeing that the heart can get in the way and that it is wicked, we should not act upon desire.

When desire enters your heart and you believe it to be godly, this is not a time to act, because the heart is deceitful above all things. Your heart may deceive you with a seemingly godly thing to fulfill your own will.

Rather than acting upon desire, even though it may appear godly, when you receive desire, it is time to pray. Every time you have a desire to do something godly, you should always lay it before the Lord. God will tell you if that is His desire for you or if it is *your* desire for you.

There is nothing we can do to please God except obey Him. Only His works can attain to all that He expects from us. Therefore let Him work through you by obedience to the Spirit, and He will be well pleased in what you do. And why? Because it is God working through you and not you yourself. God is not pleased by the works of the flesh but of the Holy Spirit.

If then you have godly desire and you desire a good thing, do not just do it, but pray. If it has already been confirmed to you that it's God's desire, that is a different situation, seeing that you are not led by desire but by confirmation. Yet it is another thing to have desire and not know for certain the heart of God.

I have had people say to me, "If it's a good thing, why should I pray? I should just do it!" But what we think is good is not always what God knows is best. It goes without saying that if we see someone starving on the street, we should just feed them. But if it's in our heart to pursue a certain path in life, we should lay it before the Lord.

Sometimes people like to use the example of delivering a suffering person to justify always walking by "godly" desire. Yet if we always know what was best at all times, then why do we still grow in the Lord? We grow because we have weakness and incomplete knowledge.

If you have any sin in your life, even just once a month, you still need growth. You know that it's wrong but don't know how to overcome it or else you wouldn't have it. We grow until we come to a full stature, being a complete and perfect creation of God. If then we are not perfect in our understanding, we should not be so quick to follow our own desires, even if they may appear godly. We should be faithful, however, to lay all things before the Lord while waiting for His answer to live by His word.

Yet when we use the example of delivering a starving person on a street to justify walking in whatever path of life we want, then there is something wrong with our hearts. If a person can't make a distinction between meeting earnest needs and choosing a path of life, then there is something wrong. But I'd rather believe it to be a sore excuse to justify a person's own desire.

We must inquire of the Lord to live by His desire and not our own. He is our master and our Lord. We must live our lives for the Lord that He may work through us. It is not what we can do for Him but what He does through us.

He doesn't need us; He never did and never will. He's been doing big things before He made this world. So why would He need our works at all? He doesn't *need* us, He *wants* us. He wants us because He loves us.

An artist doesn't need his three-year-old son to help him make a masterpiece. But an artist may *want* his three-year-old to help him make a masterpiece that he can teach his boy and have quality bonding time with him. Likewise, God wants quality bonding time with us through an intimate relationship with Him. We should submit to that by walking in the Spirit. God always knows better than us, and when we submit to Him, we please Him.

Therefore if we have desire, we must always lay it before Him first, never being anxious to do anything. Even as we said before,

> "Be anxious for nothing, but in everything by prayer and supplication, with thanksgiving, let your requests be made known to God; and the peace of God, which surpasses all understanding, will guard your hearts and minds through Christ Jesus."
>
> PHILIPPIANS 4:6–7

Be anxious for nothing but let God lead you in everything. When the Scriptures exhort us to not "be anxious," they are suggesting that whenever desire enters your heart, you should pray first and let your requests be made known to God. Afterward, His peace that surpasses all understanding will guard our hearts and minds. And why? Because when we are led by God, He is able to work through us as we wait for His word. When He works through us, we have peace in knowing that we are justified before Him.

A relationship with God requires a two-way communication. When we pray, we need to wait for Him to answer before we do anything. Prayer is a two-way radio sending messages and receiving them. We need God to communicate His message into our hearts that we may walk by obedience and faith.

Therefore guard your heart in regard to desire, and do not to step out in the flesh. Rather, wait for the Lord to answer you in order to know whether or not *He* has laid it in your heart to do a work. A good work is not always God's best work.

Therefore if it is in your heart to pursue any path of life—whether Bible college, becoming a pastor or teacher, getting married and having children, a career move, or any path you pursue in life—first lay it before God. Why shouldn't you? Anyone who says they shouldn't is afraid of God's answer. Is He not your Lord and Master? Then let *Him* dictate your life while you learn submission to His will. And if you really think He's calling you to a certain path in life, what's wrong with confirmation? Do you really think He will say no? How can you be so certain of God's will for your life if He hasn't directly spoken it to you?

Take the time to pray first. By prayer and supplication,

let your requests be made known to God. Do not be anxious for anything, but wait for Him to answer that He may lead you according to His heart. His voice is a method He uses to lead us. It is through faith in His words and His voice that we find salvation.

As it is written,

> "…faith comes by hearing, and hearing by the word of God."
>
> ROMANS 10:17

and also,

> "For by grace you have been saved through faith…"
>
> EPHESIANS 2:8

We are saved by the faith that comes from hearing His voice. Therefore take the voice of the Holy Spirit seriously. Wait for His answer in everything, and do not step out unless you step out in faith. You are not stepping out in faith unless God told you to do it. Faith comes by hearing His word and obeying it, not by thinking of a good thing to do then trying to do it without God's immediate direction.

This is an issue that plagues the church today. There are many people that seem to think that when a good work comes to mind, they should step out in faith and do it. But the Lord commands us to be anxious for nothing but to pray and wait for His word. Faith comes by His word, both oral and written. We must wait for

God to confirm His will through the Holy Spirit before we do anything, not only when it is confirmed in the pages of the Bible but also by the Holy Spirit Himself. As it is written,

> "For as many as are led by the Spirit of God, these are sons of God."
>
> ROMANS 8:14

Everything we do must be confirmed in the pages of the Bible. But it also must be confirmed through the Holy Spirit, who leads us in a daily walk with Christ, even as we read. And who do the Scriptures call the sons of God? Those who are led by the Spirit of God.

We are not even considered a son of God unless we are led by the Spirit of God. To be Christian literally means "follower of Christ." Christ leads us daily through His Spirit, and if we are not following Him, we are not following Christ. Therefore we are not Christian nor are we a son of God unless we are led by the Holy Spirit of God.

Wait for God in everything and do not be led by desire, but know what the will of the Lord is. He lays His desire in your heart that you may pray and seek His leading. Then He will speak to you, and His word shall go forth. When He has spoken to confirm His will, your faith shall come because of His word. When faith comes because His word was sent forth, it will produce the fruit of God's righteousness in you. Even as it is written,

"For as the rain comes down, and the snow from heaven, And do not return there, But water the earth, And make it bring forth and bud, That it may give seed to the sower And bread to the eater,

So shall My word be that goes forth from My mouth; It shall not return to Me void, But it shall accomplish what I please, and it shall prosper in the thing for which I sent it."

ISAIAH 55:10–11

Let the word of God prosper in you by obedience. Wait for it that you may walk by faith. When you hear the Holy Spirit, obey Him. He may guide your heart through desires He lays on your heart. But at this point, He only wants you to pray so that you may be led by His word.

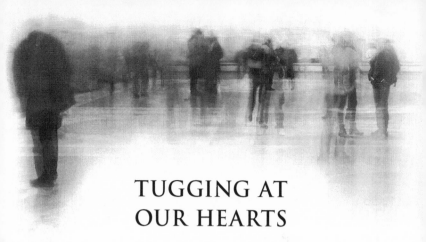

# TUGGING AT
# OUR HEARTS

ONE METHOD GOD uses to communicate with us is through inward tugs, as we briefly mentioned before. This is the Holy Spirit who is compelling us and tugging at our heart. With these "tugs," He leads and guides us throughout the day. This method, however, is more than just conviction. It is a continual leading through the day, whether in regard to situations that lead to sin or not. This tugging is His voice communicating to us through a spiritual tongue. It is by this method that He leads us in a daily walk with Christ. As we previously mentioned,

> "For as many as are led by the Spirit of God, these are sons of God."
>
> ROMANS 8:14

In this, we learn that we must be led daily in everything we do. Only those that are led by God are considered the sons of God. A Christian is a "follower of

Christ." Therefore we must take earnest heed to our walks with Him. We need to keep a focused mind on God, paying attention always to His inward "tugs." If we're not willing to be led by Him, then we cannot even be called His sons. (Or at the very least, we are not acting like His sons when we know to do better.)

He is our Lord and Master. When we came to Christ, we surrendered our life to Him that He should rule over us. Therefore we must take His leading seriously and permit Him Lordship over us. We cannot be saved by following the dictates of our own heart. Everything in the Scriptures speak against it.

But only by following the lead of the Spirit daily can we find salvation. And why? Because righteousness is faith in motion. This tug is another form of God's word, and righteousness is the application of the word of God. He is telling you through His voice (the inward pull of the Holy Spirit) what you should do, where you should go, and what you should say. And as it is written,

> "So then faith comes by hearing, and hearing by the word of God."

> ROMANS 10:17

And again,

> "For by grace you have been saved through faith, and that not of yourselves; it is the gift of God."
> EPHESIANS 2:8

We are saved by faith, which comes from His word. Therefore we are saved by believing in His word and obeying it. And as it is also written,

> "But be doers of the word, and not hearers only, deceiving yourselves."
>
> JAMES 1:22

> "But he who looks into the perfect law of liberty and continues in it, and is not a forgetful hearer but a doer of the work, this one will be blessed in what he does."
>
> JAMES 1:25

This is how we walk in the Spirit: by following the leading of the Lord. Beloved, I'd like to encourage you to become acquainted with the inward voice of the Holy Spirit. It is by His voice that He leads us, and if we want to be a Christian, then we must follow Him. You are not walking in the Spirit unless you are following Him and obeying His voice. When we walk in the Spirit, we are justified and no longer working in the flesh. As it is written,

> "I say then: Walk in the Spirit, and you shall not fulfill the lust of the flesh."
>
> GALATIANS 5:16

When we follow the Spirit daily in all things, conviction becomes easier to obey. By doing this, we are permitting God to be our strength to overcome our weaknesses.

These tugs God gives us can most easily be discerned when we sit down and put away the distractions around us. When we sit in the presence of the Lord and listen quietly, we can hear the Spirit tugging at our hearts.

Be listening to these tugs. Discern when it is the Lord, and listen to it. Even if it doesn't make sense, just follow the Lord. If you know that it's God, then why question Him? Take the time to sit in His presence to hear from Him. Obey Him, and follow His leading. It is through these tugs that He leads us daily in all things we should do.

So follow Him according to His leading. Whether you understand or not shouldn't matter. When you know that the Lord has spoken, then just obey. He knows what He's doing and has had everything planned out since before time began. He has works that are preplanned for us, and we are called to walk in them. Even as it is written,

> "For we are His workmanship, created in Christ Jesus for good works, which God prepared beforehand that we should walk in them."
>
> Ephesians 2:10

Discern His will for you. If you don't know what God wants you to be doing throughout the day, then pray for discernment and wisdom. Seek Him in prayer, and He will answer you. He will not leave you in doubt, seeing that His word saves you. It is in His heart to save you; therefore, beloved, He will always give you His word. If you're struggling with whether God will speak or not in regard to a situation, then have faith. Wait until He speaks, and do nothing until He does.

But be discerning because He may have already communicated to you what you should do in another way. Wait for His word, and when He has communicated His will to you, obey immediately. Do not wait.

When you obey immediately, you're training your heart to understand the voice of God. It gives you an opportunity to watch His words happen because of how quickly you stepped from hearing His word into fulfilling it. When you see His word fulfilled, then it increases your understanding of His voice. So take His word seriously, and walk by the Spirit.

You are saved by following His word; if you have difficulty understanding His word, He will give you the wisdom you need if you seek it. Yet remember that He is a relational God. Although He can give you what you need without your seeking it, He wants you to reach to Him first. You must seek Him for wisdom and pray for it. Then when you have extended your hand to God, He will reach back to you. Even as it is written,

> "If any of you lacks wisdom, let him ask of God,
> who gives to all liberally and without reproach,
> and it will be given to him."
>
> JAMES 1:5

Step forward in earnest prayer, and God will answer you. Seek His wisdom, and He will bless you!

When He has answered you, be submissive to His leading. If you're not continually submissive, you'll grow a callous in your heart. His voice will be difficult to hear because you chose not to listen in the first place. It's like letting a muscle go unused. What happens when you do that? It becomes weak and difficult to use. Likewise, it is difficult to use your spiritual heart muscles for following God when they go unused.

The best way to understand His leading is to practice following Him. If then you want to have a perfect walk, remember that practice makes perfect. Practice listening to God and obeying Him. The more you do this, the more you will understand Him. In order to perfect your understanding of His voice, you need to practice obeying it continually.

But when we choose to walk in the flesh and not obey His voice, it builds wax in our spiritual ears. We need to clean our ears through sitting and abiding in the Spirit. If you continuously obey Him, it will become easier for you to discern His will for you. Sometimes His will can be murky and cloudy. This usually happens under two circumstances: either when we need to grow in discernment or when we've been walking in the flesh.

If we seek to grow in understanding, God will give us what we need. If we've been walking in the flesh, then we need to repent and humble ourselves before the Lord. Then we need to sit in the secret place with the Holy Spirit, allowing Him to purify and minster to our hearts, then His voice will become easier to hear and discern.

It can be easier to hear these tugs at our hearts when we take the time to sit and abide in His presence. You need to come out from the distractions around you and sit in the secret place of the Lord. Focus on His presence, and it will be easier to hear Him. When you can hear God's voice clearly, it is easier to understand His will for you.

Make a habit of doing this daily. Also, focus on His presence throughout the day, wherever you are. When you do this with a vigilant mind, open ears, and eyes fixed on Christ, you will be able to fully understand His leading when He speaks to you.

There will always be times when it will be difficult to determine God's will. Whenever it happens, focus on the presence of the Lord by prayer and worship and with fasting if necessary. Take the time to make yourself aware of His continual presence by praying and focusing on Him throughout the day. When you feel Him with you, then begin listening to Him. At this time, His voice will be easier to discern and understand.

Be diligent to follow His lead and obey Him always. Let Him lead you to where you should go, and be willing to follow Him. In order to hear the tugs of God, you need to listen carefully, inwardly. These tugs are like small, quiet whispers. We know that God comes as a still small voice. Seeing that it is the case, we must come out from the distractions, both external and internal. Release the issues of the day to God then stop focusing on them. They can distract you from His Spirit. Focus on the presence of the Lord instead, leaving the issues of your heart behind lest your own heart should distract you from the Lord.

Hearing His small voice requires much attention, much focus, and much care. Sit forward and incline your spiritual ear to the Lord. The more you sit in His presence, the more you will understand His will for you. The more you focus on these tugs, the more you understand what you should do, what you should say, where you should go, and how you should obey.

Therefore pay earnest attention to the Lord, follow Him everywhere He leads, and obey Him in everything He calls you to do. You will be well pleasing to God, and you will understand His will for you always.

# THE UNREALIZED
# INFLUENCE OF GOD

SOMETIMES GOD LEADS us without our even knowing it. Throughout our lives, He guides us with His hand, setting up circumstances to guide our decision-making process. He does this so that we may draw nearer to Him and grope after Him in all things. He does this through circumstances in our life and through conforming our desires to His as we discussed previously.

When we have a heart like His, we tend to be led by Him without even thinking. It becomes second nature to us by the leading and guiding of the Spirit. As we grow in Him, God conforms our will to His, and by nature, we walk in His Spirit. We walk in His path and walk in His way, following Him as a force of habit.

When we continue in the Spirit, He gives us His heart. As it is written,

> "Then I will give them one heart, and I will put a new spirit within them, and take the stony heart out of their flesh, and give them a heart of flesh,

> that they may walk in My statutes and keep My
> judgments and do them; and they shall be My
> people, and I will be their God."
>
> ELZEKIEL 11:19–20

When we have His heart, rather than making decisions in our flesh according to our own heart, we seek to be pleasing to Him in all things. As it is written,

> "Therefore we make it our aim, whether present
> or absent, to be well pleasing to Him."
>
> 2 CORINTHIANS 5:9

The second way He leads us without realizing it is through the circumstances of life. Sometimes God brings things upon us to direct our thinking and decision-making, hence He is able to lead us. As it is written,

> "The king's heart is in the hand of the LORD,
> Like the rivers of water; He turns it wherever
> He wishes."
>
> PROVERBS 21:1

Similarly, this is why we are called to pray for our leaders. As we read in the Scriptures,

> "Therefore I exhort first of all that supplications,
> prayers, intercessions, and giving of thanks be
> made for all men,
>    for kings and all who are in authority, that

we may lead a quiet and peaceable life in all
godliness and reverence."

1 TIMOTHY 2:1–2

Our leaders make decisions that will affect the world
all the way up to the days of the antichrist. All nations
will we put in a place like cards on the table. God is
dealing His hand and leading those with authority to
set up the redemption of the world.

The Scriptures testify that Israel will be rebuilt as
well as the temple. In World War II, God took control
of the hearts of the Jewish people and the minds of the
world leaders. Then with one accord, He reestablished
the nation of Israel as He promised and prophesied.

Currently, the side of Jerusalem that has the temple
is occupied by the Palestinians. It is not God's timing
for the temple to be rebuilt at this moment, but when
it is, God will deal His hand, and something new will
happen. We don't know exactly what that will look
like. But we know that God is influencing the minds of
the world leaders to keep the temple from being rebuilt
prematurely. If God wanted it rebuild it, He would
force the events to happen. But for the time being, God
is relenting for His own purpose. Nevertheless, we see,
even in current events, the hand of God working to
establish the nations.

In order for the temple to be rebuilt, God will guide
the hearts of leaders again. Whether through the unfor-
tunate activity of war or through a change of political

climate, God will reestablish the temple as He promised, yet only when His perfect timing has come. Throughout the course of history, it is evident that God must have control in the hearts of men. That way, with one accord, they may fulfill what He has prophesied.

Likewise, God influences us through the circumstances of life to set us in the perfect place for finding Him. He leads us to where we shall live, when we shall have children, where and when they shall be born, where we work, and maybe even things such as where we shop for groceries. He gives us everything we need to encounter salvation.

For example: If you, who are a believer, are working at a grocery store, God may lead unbelievers to the store that they may encounter you. That way you may share the gospel in those particular circumstances for their sake. But that God leads us to draw nearer to Him is evident. As it is written,

> "...and has determined their preappointed times and the boundaries of their dwellings,
>
> so that they should seek the Lord, in the hope that they might grope for Him and find Him, though He is not far from each one of us."
>
> Act 17:26–27

God leads us that we may find Him as Savior. After we have come to know Him as Savior, He still uses the circumstances of life to lead us in the way of His will.

An example of my own life would again refer to when I met my wife.

I had moved in with a friend who didn't have a computer. Several of my bills I had to be paid online. So whenever I wanted to pay these bills, I had to go to a different friend's house. One day, very late at night, I was driving around town. I was driving aimlessly with an acquaintance when it dawned on me that I was about to be late on a bill and had to pay it that night. As I was contemplating using my friend's computer, my acquaintance coincidentally asked me, "Do you know where there's a computer I could use? I need to email someone."

So we went to the friend's house who had the computer, and there was a girl there whom I had briefly known in the past. While I waited for my turn to use the Internet, she and I began talking, and I shared my testimony with her. The Lord spoke to her in it, and she was deeply affected. We decided to get coffee together that weekend then, before a week went by, we were together.

Had I not used the computer that night, I wouldn't have married her. There was little else that would have caused us to cross paths in life. God created the circumstances of my life to meet her. I prayed specifically that He would appoint it, and the Lord set up the circumstances for me.

God also set up her circumstances as well. There was an older gentleman in need in the church who recently had moved in with my friend. He was a personal friend of hers, and she was there to visit him. Had he not recently moved in with that particular friend, she wouldn't have been there. Had he not been in need, he wouldn't have moved there. But God used the circumstances to lead us in His will. As I stated in an earlier chapter, I had recently surrendered my singleness to the Lord. I prayed for one of His daughters' hand in marriage, and He set up the circumstances to lead me to that person. It was the Lord who set it up and used the various circumstances and has continued to do so throughout our marriage.

I didn't realize God was speaking to me through the circumstances of life at that time. I didn't know it was He who was inspiring me to pay that bill that night. I never forget my bills, but somehow it slipped my mind until the last minute. I was in a rush and didn't really have a choice.

Had I not made so much as one of those decisions back then, I probably would not have my three children and my beautiful wife. So if there's anything that I've learned from that situation, it is that it is good to wait until the last minute to pay a bill.

I'm joking of course.

But whatever the case, God will always try to lead us whether we are aware of it or not. Yet we must be submissive to His guiding hand. We cannot rely on being led without knowing it, as we are called to consciously follow Him. We are called to respond to His leading and follow after Him with a willing heart.

The times that He leads us in an unbeknownst way are few and far between. This type of leading exists, but is not one that should be depended upon for a daily walk in Christ. In a daily walk, we are called to be submissive to His leading by hearing His voice and obeying it.

But there are times when God will lead you behind the scenes without your even realizing it. Seeing that we are discussing how to hear His voice and understand His leading, it is necessary to mention every method that He uses to lead us.

When He speaks to us, He communicates His will and His desire to us. But there are times when He may communicate with us without our realizing it. He will do this to guide our hearts, like the channels do the rivers of water. But nevertheless, we must open our eyes to see His guiding hand. If we pray for open eyes, God will help us see all the ways He's speaking to us and the directions He is trying to lead us.

When we don't hear God speaking, it is usually due to a lack of understanding or an issue of sin. God speaks to us in so many ways that it can be difficult to understand what He's saying if we only know one or two of the methods He uses. But if we pray for open eyes and pray for wisdom, God will grant it to us that we may understand how He is communicating to us through the course of life.

We are called to have open ears and incline them to Him that we may walk in His salvation.

As it is written,

> "Incline your ear, and come to Me. Hear, and your soul shall live; And I will make an everlasting covenant with you— The sure mercies of David."
>
> Isaiah 55:3

Knowing then that God calls us to incline our ears to Him, we ought also to grow in understanding His voice. His voice must be obeyed at all times. Rather than depending on being led in an unbeknownst way, we should have the heart to follow Him willfully and passionately at all times.

If we don't willfully follow the Lord, then we're walking in sin. We cannot live according to our own hearts or according to our flesh. We must walk in the Spirit, and the only way to walk in the Spirit is through hearing His voice and obeying. Beloved, therefore obey Him. Take your walk seriously, and the more you grow in understanding His leading, the more clearly you will hear His voice.

Open your ears to Him, and if you're having a difficult time hearing or understanding His voice, then pray for wisdom. Pursue it with your whole heart, and pray continuously. Wisdom must be a continuous pursuit. As the Lord has exhorted us through Solomon in Proverbs:

> "My son, if you receive my words, and treasure my commands within you, so that you incline

your ear to wisdom, And apply your heart to understanding;

Yes, if you cry out for discernment, And lift up your voice for understanding, If you seek her as silver, And search for her as for hidden treasures;

Then you will understand the fear of the LORD, And find the knowledge of God. For the LORD gives wisdom; From His mouth come knowledge and understanding."

PROVERBS 2:1–6

Do not be settled with a complacent life. Don't expect God to drop everything on your lap. In a relationship, two people are required to pursue one another. God has been pursuing you in His passion since before He created you. He set up the events in others' lives to lead them in finding Christ. Then He set up the events that your parents should meet and that He might form you in your mother's womb. Then He caused you to cross paths with those who shared the gospel with you. He has been pursuing you since before He made you, and you also are called to pursue God.

We came to salvation because God has been reaching for us first. Yet we are called to always be reaching back throughout our relationship with Him. We should always be reaching for Him and walking in His Spirit.

Although God may conform our desires to His that we may have a heart like His, we must not be led by desire. We still have the nature of the flesh, and we're not always perfect. Seeing then that we don't perfectly walk in the Spirit as we ought, we should not trust the desires we have. Rather, we should seek the Lord and pray whenever we have desire.

Although God may use desire to lead us in an unbeknownst way, we should not depend on it. Desire is the beginning of temptation, and our flesh often gets in the way of our relationship with Him. If we trust our heart and desires, we will walk in the flesh and not the Spirit. And that we shouldn't follow our own heart is evident. As it is written,

> "The heart is deceitful above all things, And desperately wicked; Who can know it?"
>
> JEREMIAH 17:9

Therefore do not make any decisions without Him, but be anxious for nothing. Open your eyes to His leading and pray for understanding, and He will grant it to you. But in all things, we must pray first that we may live according to the word of God. And as we stated before,

> "Be anxious for nothing, but in everything by prayer and supplication, with thanksgiving, let your requests be made known to God;
>
> and the peace of God, which surpasses all understanding, will guard your hearts and minds through Christ Jesus."
>
> PHILIPPIANS 4:6–7

Do not be led by desire but by His Holy Spirit. Grow in understanding, and the Lord will lead you in an obvious way rather than unknowingly. It is not right that we should walk with the Lord unknowingly. Rather, we should walk with Him in full consciousness, being vigilant of mind and sincere in heart.

# HAVING PASSION
# FOR CHRIST

In order to hear the voice of God more effectively we need to take affirmative actions in our walk. We must to take a walk with Him seriously, listening to His Spirit and obeying Him continuously. If we do not continuously obey we are not going to hear Him as well. If we choose to walk in sin, and ignore conviction, conviction may stop altogether until we repent.

If you're plugging your fingers in your spiritual ears, then you're not going to hear God. There are some who do this, purposefully ignoring God while they walk according to their own heart, justifying it. But if you willfully submit to the leading of the Holy Spirit, you will be able to hear Him clearly and effectively. The more you practice this, the better you'll hear Him.

If you want to grow in understanding the voice the Lord, the best way is through prayer and alone time spent with God. In order to gain understanding, we must have fervent hearts for growth. We must ask God to increase our knowledge of Him, and He will answer us. As it is written,

> "…Yet you do not have because you do not ask."
>
> JAMES 4:2

Some people feel that if they only ask, they will receive. Yet we must also seek, stepping forward to receive it. In this, God sees your heart and will give you what you approach by faith. Asking itself isn't seeking; taking affirmative actions is seeking.

Some of these actions are: passionately pursuing Him on a daily basis, seeking to grow in a walk with Him, praying for understanding, growing in the knowledge of the Word, and being still and listening intently to the Spirit then obeying Him immediately.

If we love the Lord, we'll show Him our passion through a walk with Him. But how can we know to rightly walk unless we know how to rightly divide His word? As it is written,

> "Be diligent to present yourself approved to God, a worker who does not need to be ashamed, rightly dividing the word of truth."
>
> 2 TIMOTHY 2:15

All things the Holy Spirit actively speaks to you can be backed up by Scripture. God never contradicts Himself. We must be diligent to present ourselves approved to

God and to please Him. But how do the Scriptures say that we are found approved by Him? Through knowing how to rightly divide the word of truth.

When you grow in the Scriptures, you will grow in understanding the voice of God. If you think that God has spoken to you, you should compare it to the Scriptures. Everything God speaks will line up with His word. Seeing that this is the case, the more you understand the Scriptures and the perfect truth of the doctrine, the more you will understand the voice of God.

Spend more time with Him, having more than a devotion with Him. It's good to have a devotion, but do more than this and dive deep in the Scriptures. Come to understand your Bible. Many Christians believe that they do understand the perfect one true doctrine, but then the question remains, "Why are there so many different beliefs on any one given topic?"

We as Christians are too focused on our own opinions. Beloved, I would like to encourage you to let go of your own opinion and seek the heart of God. Examine your own heart at this time, and ask yourself honestly, "Am I opinionated with my beliefs?" or "Am I seeking the opinions of others rather than seeking the opinion of God?"

God's opinion is perfect truth. We need to stop asking one another, "What's your take on this scripture?" or "What do you make of this scripture? What's your opinion?" Beloved, God's opinion is all that matters. He will judge us according to His opinion. The judgment we receive from God will be based from His own heart. If we want to be pleasing Him in regard to His judgment, then we must consider His opinion and not that of others or our own.

Therefore take it seriously, and seek God's opinion and not that of others. Seek His perfect truth, and His Holy Spirit will guide you to it. If you have an open mind with God, you'll have open spiritual ears. We need to have an open mind when asking God to reveal the meaning behind the Scriptures to us because He may say something that we do not expect. Yet His word is perfect truth and perfect doctrine.

There is only one doctrine and one truth. Yet many believe different things about the same subject. We are called by the Lord to be of the same mind and of the same judgment. Why? Because there is only one God, one way of salvation, one truth, one Name by which we are saved, and only one Savior.

Knowing this to be true, we must take our walks seriously and seek the Lord in truth, being careful to abstain from the opinions of men. Yes, there are some who may understand the doctrine whose teachings can be listened to, and God will speak through them. However, in regard to seeking opinions, we ought to abstain from the interpretations of men and instead ask God to interpret His own word.

We must take our walks seriously. We must take the doctrine seriously. Do not be complacent, but be passionate.

As it is written,

> "For the turning away of the simple will slay them,
> And the complacency of fools will destroy them;
> But whoever listens to me will dwell safely,
> and will be secure, without fear of evil."
>
> PROVERBS 1:32–33

And that we should be diligent to obey His voice is evident. For it is written,

> "…Today, if you will hear His voice: Do not harden your hearts, as in the rebellion…"
>
> PSALM 95:7–8

But that paying attention to doctrine and abiding in the one truth saves us is evident. For it is written,

> "Take heed to yourself and to the doctrine. Continue in them, for in doing this you will save both yourself and those who hear you."
>
> 1 TIMOTHY 4:16

And that improper doctrine leads astray and kills is evident. For it is written,

> "You ran well. Who hindered you from obeying the truth?
> This persuasion does not come from Him who calls you. A little leaven leavens the whole lump."
>
> GALATIANS 5:7–9

And also,

> "Brethren, if anyone among you wanders from the truth, and someone turns him back,
>
> let him know that he who turns a sinner from the error of his way will save a soul from death and cover a multitude of sins."
>
> James 5:19–20

Do you understand what this scripture in James is declaring? That if anyone doesn't walk in truth, their soul abides in death! Beloved, take it as a most serious thing. God's word cannot be taught any other way! It says what it says, and the word of God must be believed and obeyed! We can't just pick and choose what we like in the Scriptures. Yet some take certain scriptures to justify their standpoint then throw out the rest. When they're rebuked with other scriptures that stand against their beliefs, they say, "God didn't really mean that," or, "The scriptures aren't really saying that; they're saying if you could abide in death." They always use the statement "If this or that could happen." But read the scripture in James! It doesn't say, "If you could" anywhere in that verse. Their statement is an interpretation of men added to the gospel according to their opinion. Our faith must be in what is written, not in what men interpret. It must be in what God speaks and interprets to us through His Holy Spirit, who enlightens our understanding of the word. It is the Lord who opens our understanding of His word and His gospel. As it is written,

"And He opened their understanding, that they might comprehend the Scriptures."

LUKE 24:45

God teaches us His doctrine through His Holy Spirit. His Spirit may speak through others that you may know His doctrine, as each one has received a gift from God. Some men have received from the Lord to be a pastor or preacher and speak through the Holy Spirit. When you learn how to discern the voice of God, you will feel God speaking through them, even if it's not something you previously knew. In this, God has established teachers of His doctrine in His church that you may walk by the truth. Therefore, beloved, become acquainted with the voice of God, and take it as a most serious thing. His Holy Spirit leads us to all perfect truth. As we read,

"However, when He, the Spirit of truth, has come, He will guide you into all truth..."

JOHN 16:13

If then we seek the truth, we also seek the Lord Jesus. For it is written,

"Jesus said to him, 'I am the way, the truth, and the life. No one comes to the Father except through Me.'"

JOHN 14:6

Jesus is the truth, and to walk in Him and the way of His truth is to walk in life. Those who do not follow after the Lord in truth cannot be saved. For He is the truth and the life, and if we do not walk in His truth, we do not walk in the way of life.

We can't walk however we think is best or however we feel and still believe that we have the salvation God gives. His salvation comes through His one and only Gospel. If we believe in anything else, faith does not save us. And why? Because our faith is no longer in the word of God but in the words and opinions of men, and men do not save. Only by Jesus Christ are we saved, and only by His name are we delivered. But what happens to those that teach a different doctrine and are complacent in preaching truth? As we read,

> "I marvel that you are turning away so soon from Him who called you in the grace of Christ, to a different gospel, which is not another; but there are some who trouble you and want to pervert the gospel of Christ.
>
> But even if we, or an angel from heaven, preach any other gospel to you than what we have preached to you, let him be accursed. As we have said before, so now I say again, if anyone preaches any other gospel to you than what you have received, let him be accursed."
>
> GALATIANS 1:6–9

We must take His word seriously in reverence of the Lord. We must fear and love the Lord. We can't walk in any pattern we think is best and expect grace. We must walk according to the pattern delivered to us from the Lord in the Scriptures. We must take the word of God seriously. We are led by His word, both written and orally spoke by the Spirit, who wrote the Scriptures. But if we don't follow the word in truth, then we don't follow Christ in truth, and Christian literally means "follower of Christ." If we don't understand His doctrine, we won't understand His voice when He speaks.

Although we may be able to understand His voice from time to time, we will not be able to perfectly understand it until we perfectly understand His doctrine. His word shows us how He leads us and speaks to us. When we come to know His word, it is easier to understand His leading. If then you want a perfect walk with Him, walk in love and pure doctrine. Seek the truth, and live according to it. Take it seriously, and He will bless you with a deeper, more fulfilling, and more enriching relationship with Him.

Spend more time with Him. Sit in His presence throughout the day, turning your ears inwardly at all times. Constantly listen to the Holy Spirit. When you grow in the word and continually practice obeying God, His voice will become clearer to you and easier to understand. When you understand His voice, it's easier to follow Him.

There are many things that will distract you. For example, the duties of your workplace may distract you from the Lord. However, you can focus on the presence of the Spirit and the necessities of the day at the same time. As you practice this, you will grow in it. The more you grow in it, the easier it will be to do throughout the day. It's like exercising a muscle. The more you exercise it, the more it is able to overcome difficult things.

Beloved, be diligent to seek the Lord. The more you seek Him, the greater your relationship with Him will be. If you want to hear His voice more clearly, then hold Him more dearly. Get closer to Him, and you will hear His still, small voice better.

Be passionate in all that you do, and be diligent to obey. Follow through with love, and continue in His word. In doing these things, you will not only please Him but understand Him better. When you understand His voice, you can hear Him more clearly, being able to more accurately discern when He has spoken. When you hear His voice more clearly, you can understand how to obey it more effectively. These go hand in hand, but you can only grow in them through growing in a relationship with Him and being diligent to obey immediately. Obey everything God speaks to you, whether conviction, compelling, leading, or things He teaches you through the Scriptures for a daily walk.

Be closer to Him in the word, and you will be closer to Him in the end. His Bible is His private journal. When you understand His journal, you will understand the heart of the Person who wrote it. While you're reading the Bible, God will speak to you in the Scriptures. When the words of the pages pop out to you, this is the Lord speaking to you. Write down what He teaches you, and memorize the scriptures He points out to you. When you write down what He teaches you, you're practicing listening to the voice of God. Every time you hear God when you read, write what He says. In this, you have an opportunity to practice listening to and hearing God. Remember that practice makes perfect! If you practice listening, you will perfect your understanding of His voice. By doing this, it will help you grow in understanding His voice. It will, in fact, help you in every area of life and not reading only.

Have passion for the Lord. Be diligent to seek Him. Read His word, and write what He teaches you. Memorize the Scriptures that speak out to you, for the Lord wants you to do so, having pointed them out to you. Love Him by obedience. In doing these things, His voice will be easier to understand, and you'll hear Him more clearly.